SHARING THE
WORLD WITH ANIMALS

Published by Creative Education, 123 South Broad Street, Mankato, Minnesota 56001

Copyright © 1996 by Wildlife Education, Ltd. Copyright 1996 hardbound edition by Creative Education. All rights reserved. No part of this book may be reproduced in any form without written permission from the publisher. Printed in the United States.

Printed by permission of Wildlife Education, Ltd.

Library of Congress Cataloging-in-Publication Data

Shaw, Marjorie B.
Sharing the world with animals / series created by John Bonnet Wexo; written by Marjorie B. Shaw; zoological consultant, Charles R. Schroeder; scientific consultant, Charles Radcliffe.
p. cm. — (Zoobooks)
Includes index.
Summary: Discusses how life is supported by the earth and how everything living is inter-related and co-dependent on the life cycle.
ISBN 0-88682-778-7
1. Ecology—Juvenile literature. 2. Man—Influence on nature—Juvenile literature.
[1. Ecology. 2. Man—Influence on nature.] I. Title. II. Series: Zoo books (Mankato, Minn.)
QH541.14.S48 1996
574.5—dc20   95-49375   CIP AC

SHARING THE
WORLD WITH ANIMALS

Creative Education

Art Credits

Darrel Millsap

Pages Thirteen, Fourteen, Fifteen, and Sixteen: Richard Orr

Photographic Credits

Front Cover: Phil A. Dotson (*Photo Researchers*)

Page Six: Upper Right, Francisco Erize (*Bruce Coleman, Ltd.*); **Middle Left,** Michael Fogden (*DRK Photo*); **Lower Right,** Marc and Evelyn Bernheim (*Woodfin Camp*)

Page Seven: Upper Right, Stephen J. Krasemann (*DRK Photo*); **Middle Right,** Larry Lipsky (*Tom Stack & Associates*); **Bottom,** J. Hobday (*Natural Science Photos*)

Page Eight: Cristina Smith (*Wildlife Education, Ltd.*)

Page Nine: Scott Blackmar (*Tom Stack & Associates*)

Page Ten: Upper Right, Nicholas Devore III (*Bruce Coleman, Inc.*); **Lower Right,** Charles Mauzy (*Allstock*)

Page Twelve: Middle Left, Mark Boulton (*Bruce Coleman, Ltd.*); **Middle Right,** Gerry Ellis (*Ellis Wildlife*)

Page Seventeen: Upper Right, G. Douglas (*FPG International*); **Middle Right,** Don Riepe (*Peter Arnold, Inc.*); **Lower Left,** Gary Milburn (*Tom Stack & Associates*)

Page Eighteen: Upper Right, Thase Daniel (*Bruce Coleman, Inc.*); **Lower Right,** Gerry Ellis (*Ellis Wildlife*)

Page Nineteen: August Upitus (*FPG International*)

Page Twenty-One: Middle Left and Right, John Oldenkamp (*Wildlife Education, Ltd.*)

Page Twenty-Two: Middle Left, Esther Beaton (*Auscape International*); **Lower Left,** Cristina Smith (*Wildlife Education, Ltd.*); **Lower Right,** John Oldenkamp (*Wildlife Education, Ltd.*)

Page Twenty-Three: Upper Left, John Oldenkamp (*Wildlife Education, Ltd.*); **Upper Middle and Lower Right,** Cristina Smith (*Wildlife Education, Ltd.*)

Our Thanks To: Elizabeth Lipscomb (*U.S. Fish and Wildlife Service*); Grace Magee (*CRES*); Lydia Anderson (*World Wildlife Fund*); Wendy Perkins, Valerie Hare, Linda Coates (*San Diego Zoo Library*); Michael Clark; Mission Hills Nursery; Casey and Lizzie Elwood; Tyler Burch; Conor Mongan; Enrique Newcomb; Maya Satz; Natasha Wood; Joe Selig

Cover Photo: Bobcat

Contents

Near the cold South Pole, in 1984, scientists discovered a widening hole in the ozone layer of the upper atmosphere, or *stratosphere*. This layer protects Earth's inhabitants from the searing ultraviolet rays of the sun. The hole in the ozone is caused by events taking place half a world away.

The rain forest is a delicate ecosystem. Its decline or survival affects all the world. When the forest is cut down, Earth's chemical balance changes.

Earth is a small and fragile world. Does this surprise you? Earth, with its vast distances, is the only planet in the universe that is *known* to support life. Life began on Earth billions of years ago and developed into millions of *species*, or kinds, of plants and animals. Why then, with all this life and space, is Earth fragile?

It is because all of nature is connected — all living things depend on one another for survival. When an animal species becomes extinct, it affects the other animals linked to it — its predators and its prey — and the balance of nature is disturbed. When the environment or an *ecosystem* — a community of animals and plants that share the same environment — is greatly altered in one part of the world, it also affects other parts of the world. That is why we must all learn to *share* the world.

Grasslands usually are hot and fairly dry, with only scattered trees. In Africa, giraffes, antelope, lions and other predators share this ecosystem with nomadic tribesmen grazing their cattle. If too many domestic cattle graze in one area, it destroys the land for the wild species.

Life in the ocean is as varied as life on land. Fish, marine mammals, seabirds, and people who earn their living from the sea depend on a healthy, unpolluted ocean for their existence.

People often think of wetlands as wasted land that could be better used. They drain marshes for farmland, housing tracts, or freeways. But wetlands are breeding and feeding grounds for many animals. Destroying wetlands reduces wildlife and increases flooding.

Although too dry for most life, deserts are home to animals that need little water. Some *people* have learned to survive in the desert, like the Bedouins in the Sahara and the Bushmen of the Kalahari.

A **tree and the animals** that live in and around it form a *biotic community*—a self-sustaining living system of plants and animals sharing a common habitat. All living things in this community depend on one another and on the nonliving essentials of their environment—air, water, soil, and the sun. This small community is an example of how living things interact with each other and with their environment in the larger world.

A *food chain* is one way the community is connected. In the food chain, the tree is a *producer*. It depends on the sun for the energy to grow. In the process, it produces food for the animals in the community. The animals that eat the leaves and nuts from the tree are *primary consumers*. Animals that eat primary consumers are called *secondary consumers*. *Decomposers* are the forms of life in the community that convert dead plants and animals into *nutrients*, or food, for the soil. In turn, the nutritious soil helps the tree to grow.

The tree uses water, then releases it into the air through its leaves. This is called *transpiration*. The water released eventually becomes rain, which provides water for thirsty plants and animals.

The acorn woodpecker pecks holes in the oak tree. It then uses the holes to store acorns from the tree, so it can eat later on. The tree provides food and storage space to the bird. The acorn woodpecker is a primary consumer.

Squirrels also eat acorns from the tree and are primary consumers. Sometimes, if the bobcat in the area is fast enough, it may catch and eat one of the squirrels. The bobcat is a secondary consumer.

The roots of a tree act as a "sponge" to hold water in the soil. As rain falls and soaks the earth, the roots draw up the water and release it slowly and steadily to the tree.

Through its roots, the tree takes up the nutrients in the enriched soil. The nutrients help the tree produce more acorns for squirrels and woodpeckers. And some of the squirrels will become food for a new generation of bobcats.

A caterpillar eats oak leaves. It, too, is a primary consumer.

A flicker, another kind of wood-pecker, digs a hole in the tree for a nest. The flicker eats insects, not acorns. It is a secondary consumer because it eats the caterpillar that eats the oak leaves. Without the tree, there would be no caterpillar for the flicker to eat!

Oxygen and carbon dioxide are both gases that are necessary to life on Earth. Plants like the oak tree provide oxygen for animals, including people, to breathe. When we breathe out, or *exhale*, we give off carbon dioxide, which the oak tree and other plants take in. Carbon dioxide is as important to plants as oxygen is to us. Plants can't live without animals, and animals can't live without plants.

OXYGEN

CARBON DIOXIDE

The cycle of life and death maintains balance in the tree and its community. When plants or animals die, they decompose and turn into nutrients that other plants and animals live on.

When a bobcat or other animal dies, bacteria and other tiny organisms break down the body cells and the animal decomposes. Chemicals in the cells are recycled into the soil.

After insects, bacteria, molds, and fungi—all decomposers —have played their part in the cycle, the soil is rich with nutrients that help the tree to grow.

FUNGI

Can you imagine how a biotic community or an ecosystem changes when people clear the forest or start forest fires? Animals lose food and shelter, and the ecological community is destroyed. Soil washes away with no roots to hold it. Without soil, new trees can't grow. And new soil is only created through the interaction of living organisms. Soil developed over thousands of years can be lost in a few years. It will take a long time for a new community to form—maybe several hundred years. Now, imagine loggers that work to keep the forest secure. Instead of bulldozers that strip the soil, these loggers use draft horses to remove logs *selectively*. The biotic community remains, and the loggers and local craftsmen and furniture makers have work. These people act responsibly toward their environment and are a part of the natural community.

9

The world and its wild places are under a lot of pressure. And although the pressure takes many forms, the basic problem is overpopulation. Too many people drive too many cars, use too many pesticides, overcrowd the planet, pollute the air and water, and strip the soil of its nutrients. All of these things make the world unhealthy for all life — city dwellers and creatures of the shrinking wilderness.

These are all *new* problems for the world, problems that developed during this century. The rise of industry and technology that improved living conditions for many people also separated those people from nature. Increased industrialization continued to make life easier for many humans, but caused hardships for other species.

It was a long time before people realized that nature was being abused. It was longer still before they realized that what affected nature also affected them. Now, people are becoming aware that they are part of nature. Many are trying to heal the Earth. Repairing the damage is possible, but requires the efforts of us all.

When cars burn fuel, they give off carbon, which causes pollution. Burning fossil fuels and cutting down forests both increase carbon dioxide in the atmosphere. Carbon dioxide has a life-span of 500 years. This and other gases cause the "greenhouse effect," which over-warms the world. When this happens, the climatic balance is changed and affects all life.

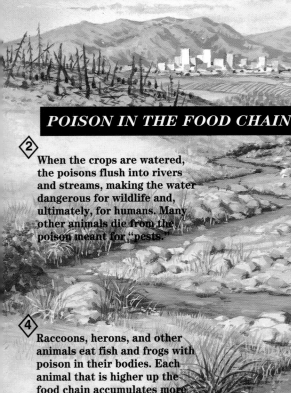

POISON IN THE FOOD CHAIN

①
So there will be more unblemished, pest-free fruit and vegetables, farmers use planes to dust crops with poisons that kill pests and weeds.

②
When the crops are watered, the poisons flush into rivers and streams, making the water dangerous for wildlife and, ultimately, for humans. Many other animals die from the poison meant for "pests."

④
Raccoons, herons, and other animals eat fish and frogs with poison in their bodies. Each animal that is higher up the food chain accumulates more poison in its body. Those at the top of the food chain get the most poison.

③
The fish that live in the stream eat tiny poisoned plants and animals. Poisons from the water are stored in their bodies and will eventually kill them.

Water and soil are Earth's most important resources. When trees are cut down, there is nothing to bind the soil and it is washed away, or *erodes*. The exposed ground dries and cracks, and streams shrink and change their nature. In a stream thick with eroded dirt, sunlight can't reach underwater plants. Many of them die.

The ozone layer of the atmosphere protects all life from the burning ultraviolet rays of the sun. Too much exposure to those rays can cause skin cancer. Without ozone, the life-giving sun would be deadly. *Chlorofluorocarbons*, or CFCs — chemicals we release into the atmosphere daily — damage the ozone layer.

Some products that make life more convenient for us, like spray cans and styrofoam food containers, give off CFCs that eat up the ozone. Every molecule of CFC releases chlorine atoms, each of which can destroy 100,000 molecules of ozone. Fortunately, since 1988, CFCs in the atmosphere have declined. With new laws to halt production of CFCs in many countries, the ozone layer may begin to recover by the year 2005.

Chemicals in factory smoke are carried far away by winds. They combine with water and other pollutants in the atmosphere and fall to earth as "acid" rain, which has a high level of sulfur and nitrogen. Instead of a rainfall that promotes growth and nourishes plants, this highly acidic rain causes trees and other plants to wither and die.

POPULATION PRESSURES

It took many thousands of years for the world population to hit the one billion mark. That was in 1800. Less than 200 years later there are more than 5½ billion people in the world. Of those people, more than 2½ billion were born since 1960! Such a population explosion overwhelms the world.

Nature has a limited ability to renew itself and recover from abuse. Every crime against nature — the pollution of air and water, the extinction of animal and plant species, deforestation, global warming — is linked to overpopulation.

If the population continues to grow at its present rate, by 2150 — during the lifetimes of your great grandchildren — the world population will be *694 billion*. But the planet can't support that many. Today's tragedies would be multiplied by billions.

The population pressures can be reversed if people limit their families to one or two children. From now until you are teenagers and young adults is the most critical time to reverse the population explosion. People all over the world must learn that overpopulation is the greatest danger to the Earth. The planet will simply run out of resources.

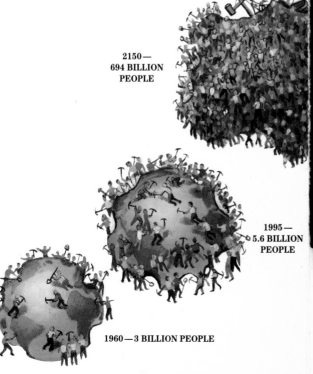

2150 —
694 BILLION
PEOPLE

1995 —
5.6 BILLION
PEOPLE

1960 — 3 BILLION PEOPLE

1930 — 2 BILLION PEOPLE

1800 — 1 BILLION PEOPLE

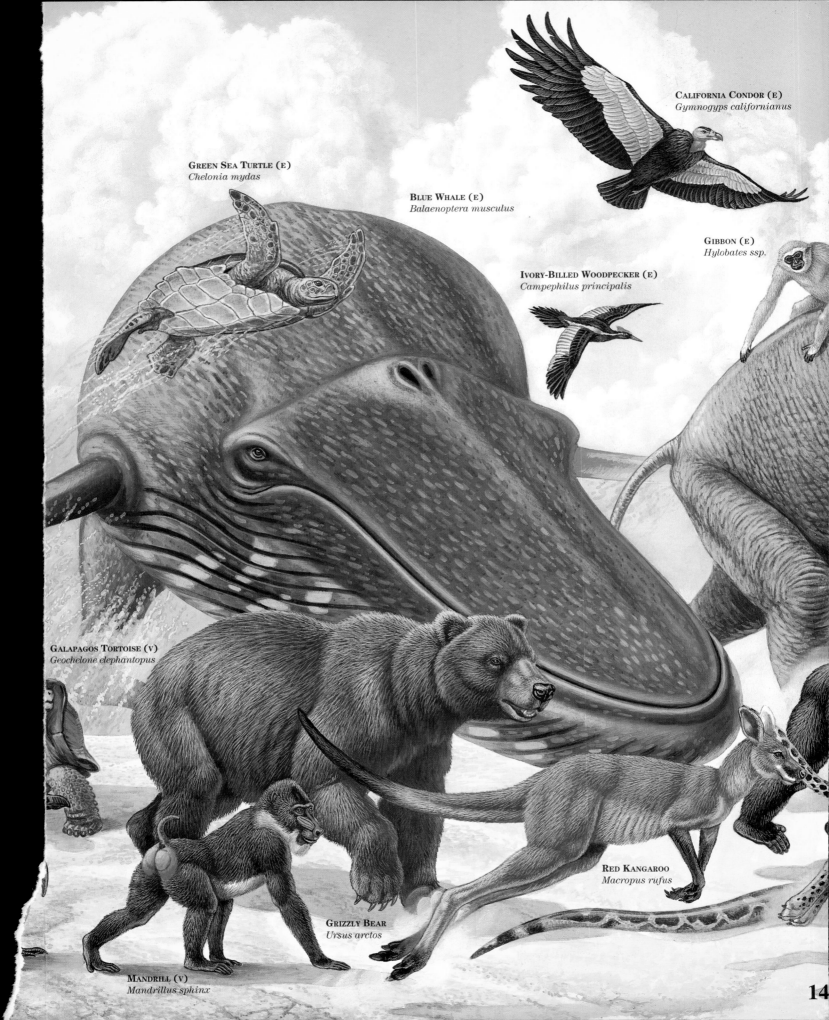

CALIFORNIA CONDOR (E)
Gymnogyps californianus

GREEN SEA TURTLE (E)
Chelonia mydas

BLUE WHALE (E)
Balaenoptera musculus

GIBBON (E)
Hylobates ssp.

IVORY-BILLED WOODPECKER (E)
Campephilus principalis

GALAPAGOS TORTOISE (V)
Geochelone elephantopus

RED KANGAROO
Macropus rufus

GRIZZLY BEAR
Ursus arctos

MANDRILL (V)
Mandrillus sphinx

14

People wearing animal skins and teeth probably don't think they have caused animals to die — but they have. People that buy clothes and jewelry made from exotic animals *create* an opportunity for poachers to earn money by illegally killing animals. If there were no one to buy clothes of animal skins, it wouldn't be worthwhile to kill the animals.

The clothes worn by the man and woman on this page represent 10 animals killed for fashion. The woman's hat and coat are made from leopard skins, and her boots and handbag are snakeskin.

Many nations are part of an agreement called the Convention on International Trade in Endangered Species, or CITES, for short. Those countries that sign the pact agree not to sell or import any products made from endangered animals and plants. It is illegal to bring any of these products into the United States. But some still come into the country illegally.

Prehistoric people wore animal skins because it was the only clothing they had. Today, people can buy clothes of many fabrics and man-made materials. People don't even look good in animal skins. The skins look best when they are healthy, sleek and supple, and *on* the animal!

In the United States, 17 million wild animals are trapped each year as pests or for their skins. When the trap slams shut, it feels like a car door slamming on your hand. But the animal can't open the trap to release its paw.

It doesn't matter to poachers that snow leopards are endangered animals. They kill snow leopards for money so the skins can be made into coats.

Baby harp seals are killed for their skins to make jackets like the one this man is wearing. Their mothers try to protect the babies, but are no match for the seal hunters.

This man is stepping on the alligator in more ways than one. His boots are made from alligator skin. Thousands of alligators are killed every year just for their skins.

Hundreds of elephants were killed just for these tusks. In countries that don't have endangered species laws, these tusks will be made into ivory jewelry and art objects. The woman at right is wearing ivory earrings and an ivory bracelet. If she tries to bring them into the United States, they will be confiscated by the authorities at customs. She spent her money for nothing.

On these panels are some animals which are now extinct (EX) and many that are endangered (E) or vulnerable (V). A few on the right panel were rescued at the very edge of extinction. Some of them occur in adequate numbers only in zoos or preserves. They are still considered endangered in the wild. All efforts to build a sustainable population of the whooping crane are failing. This stately American bird seems doomed to extinction. Those animals with no code following their names are in no imminent danger.

GUADALUPE STORM PETREL (EX)
Oceanodroma macrodactyla

STELLER'S SEA COW (EX)
Hydrodamalis gigas

PASSENGER PIGEON (EX)
Extopistes migratorius

PINK-HEADED DUCK (EX)
Rhodonessa caryophyllacea

SCHOMBURGK'S DEER (EX)
Cervus schomburgki

AUROCHS (EX)
Bos primigenius

QUAGGA (EX)
Equus quagga

BARBARY LION (EX)
Panthera leo leo

TASMANIAN WOLF (EX)
Thylacinus cynocephalus

ELEPHANT BIRD (EX)
Aepyornis maximus

GREAT AUK (EX)
Alca impennis

People use *petroleum*, a fossil fuel, to heat their homes, to provide energy for industry, and to run our automobiles. As more and more countries industrialize, more of this oil is taken from the Earth. But petroleum is a *non-renewable resource*. Eventually the Earth's supply won't be able to meet the demand, and the world will run out of oil. It's important that people develop other fuels that are also less polluting.

Cars pollute less that get more miles to the gallon. Reformulated gasoline further reduces pollution. Many people in Los Angeles have used reformulated gas since 1990. The city's cars have almost doubled in the past 25 years, but the smog has decreased by more than 50 percent!

When tankers carrying oil leak accidentally, oil pollutes the water, and animals suffer. Fur and feathers soaked with oil cannot keep animals warm. Sea otters try to lick off the oil, and it poisons them.

Oil spills also kill the tiny animals and plants that sea animals eat. Crabs covered with oil usually will not survive. If they do, their flesh is poisonous to animals that eat them. The poison from the oil travels through the food chain.

Every year, Americans produce 290 million tons of toxic waste. Usually, the wastes are put in a dump. But they seep into the ground water. Animals that drink the water are poisoned.

A more chronic, and more serious, cause of oil-polluted waters comes from oil tankers filled with sea water! On the way to their "filling stations," the ships need *ballast* to keep them stable. They can't go with empty tanks, so they fill up with sea water as ballast. The ballast water becomes contaminated with residual oil in the tanks. When the tankers reach their destinations, the ballast water is flushed into lagoons. This common practice accounts for most of the 890 million gallons of oil that pollute marine environments every year. The occasional major oil spill deposits 9 or 10 million gallons. Treating ballast water would decrease oil pollution.

WHOOPING CRANE (E)
Grus americana

TRUMPETER SWAN
Cygnus buccinator

EUROPEAN BISON (V)
Bison bonasus

TULE ELK
Cervus canadensis

WHITE-TAILED GNU (V)
Connochaetes gnou

HAWAIIAN GOOSE (V)
Branta sandvicensis

SIBERIAN TIGER (E)
Panthera tigris altaica

QUEENSLAND HAIRY-NOSED WOMBAT (E)
Lasiorhinus krefftii

16

ORIENTAL WHITE STORK (E)
Ciconia ciconia boyciana

AFRICAN ELEPHANT (V)
Loxodonta africana

GREAT INDIAN RHINOCEROS (E)
Rhinoceros unicornis

MONGOLIAN WILD HORSE (E)
Equus przewalskii

CHIMPANZEE (V)
Pan troglodytes

GALAPAGOS FUR SEAL
Arctocephalus galapagoensis

MOUNTAIN GORILLA (E)
Gorilla gorilla beringei

CHEETAH (E)
Acinonyx jubatus

INDIAN PYTHON (V)
Python molurus molurus

AMERICAN CROCODILE (E)
Crocodylus acutus

15

Nature can heal itself—if we let it. First, we must stop overburdening the Earth and its resources. Since the Endangered Species Act of 1973, other laws and regulations were passed. They assured cleaner air and water, and banished some harmful pesticides, like DDT. These laws worked. Many endangered species replenished their numbers, and the air and water is cleaner. It is important to keep these laws.

Now that the environment is recovering, it's up to humans to keep it healthy. Many scientists and volunteers work to improve the environment. But governments have conflicting issues that require attention. Programs to help nature often get set aside. Let governments know that the environment needs a high priority. We are a part of nature. What happens to the environment affects our future.

If sick streams become healthy again, they can provide homes for many animals. One simple way to save a stream is to bring in beavers to build dams. This helps to stop soil erosion so plants can grow that animals will eat. This is nature healing itself—with a little help from us.

Beaver dams block eroded soil from traveling downstream. They also trap water in ponds, which raises the level of water in the ground. As material decomposes in beaver ponds, nutrients recycle so that tiny plants and animals can use them. The food chain now has a fresh start.

In China, special land is set aside for pandas. Approximately 1,000 pandas remain in the wild. Many have succumbed to shrinking habitat and the natural die-off of bamboo, which they eat almost exclusively. Animal reserves to protect one species also benefit many other species—including humans. When forests are preserved, all the forest dwellers keep their habitats. By saving trees, we save soil, and that prevents erosion and flooding.

People are restoring streams so that salmon can again migrate upstream to lay their eggs. Streams die when there is too much logging and mining nearby. Other streams are blocked by dams. These things keep salmon from reproducing. Making new passages for the salmons' journey also assures a food supply for animals that eat salmon.

Peregrine falcons became endangered because they lost wilderness habitat and they are high on the food chain. They couldn't withstand the accumulated poisons in their prey. Many peregrines were saved when scientists moved them to cities! For these, their wilderness cliffs are now city skyscrapers. They are safe from larger birds of prey, and they have city-dwelling pigeons to eat.

Sometimes, when it seems there is no hope for an animal in the wild, zoos can save a species through captive breeding. Zoo programs may have saved condors from extinction. Eggs collected in the wild were hatched and raised at the zoo.

When migrating birds fly into power lines, they are sometimes killed by electricity. One way to keep this from happening is to bury power lines in the ground. Many communities have underground power now. It helps the birds, and it looks nicer to humans.

To convince the young birds that they were condors, keepers hid themselves and fed the chicks with a condor puppet. The ultimate goal of captive-breeding programs for endangered species is that conditions in nature will improve enough to return the species to the wild.

19

Getting in touch with nature is the first step to discovering how all living things are connected to each other and to the environment. Start to notice the plants and animals around you, the sky, the flowers, the trees. Listen to the birds, watch the wind move the clouds. Watch nesting birds from a safe distance so you don't frighten the birds.

You can help clean up the environment for yourself and your animal friends. And you can create new habitats for them. It doesn't matter where you live, you can still give a home to an animal — even if it is a small one. You can make a habitat in your backyard or even on a windowsill. Just by growing a plant or two, you can provide food and shelter for animals. By beginning in your own backyard, you may spark an idea that spreads through the neighborhood to the whole community!

You might plant a tree with some friends or with your family. The tree will provide food and shelter for animals. And it will help filter out pollution. One acre of sycamore trees could capture 15 tons of pollutants a year.

Make it a habit to pick up litter in the park or along the street. Animals can get caught in plastic bags. And they can eat litter that is bad for them.

PLEASE DON'T LITTER

Quietly watch animals to learn how they live. Knowing animal habits is a key to saving them. One day, you might even be a scientist who works to save animals or protect the environment.

Bats are losing their natural habitats, so they need new homes in order to survive. You can help by building a bat box. To find out how to make a bat box, write to Bat Conservation International, P. O. Box 162603, Austin, TX 78716.

Make a rock pile for lizards. They will then have a safe place to hide from predators. Lizards are good friends to have in your garden. They eat the insects that eat your plants.

Eastern bluebirds and many other birds are losing their nesting sites to shopping malls. But they don't need to be homeless—you can build them a house. To learn how to build a bluebird house, write to North American Bluebird Society, P. O. Box 6295, Silver Spring, MD 20906-0295.

By planting flowers in your backyard, you can create your own biotic community. First, you will dig the soil that carries nutrients to so many living things. Your flowers will attract bees, butterflies, and birds. In winter, birds eat the seeds that are left behind when flowers die. Use native plants when you can—they belong in your community. Watch your garden through the seasons to see how the natural cycles work in a small ecosystem. You will discover how nice it feels to be a part of the nature that surrounds you.

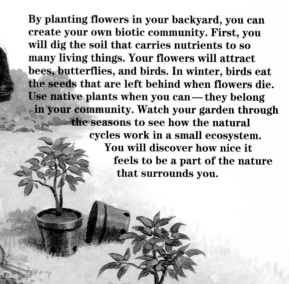

You can create a small ecosystem by growing flowers in a window box or flower pot. The flowers will attract insects and birds and will provide food for them. You can also put out a bird feeder. This will help keep city birds from starving in the winter.

The world is your home. Make it safe for you and the creatures that share it, by changing some habits. Automobiles are polluting necessities. But if yours gets good gas mileage and you share rides to reduce the traffic on the road, you've helped the environment. Where there is good mass transportation, use it when you can.

Recycle paper products, glass, aluminum cans, and plastic. This saves trees, energy, and landfills. To avoid polluting the soil and ground water, take paint and kerosene cans, used batteries, and other toxic wastes to a hazardous waste collection center. If you don't have a recycling program in your community, start one, or convince the city or county to start one.

Conserve water all the time, not just when there's a drought. Instead of hosing off the sidewalk, sweep it with a broom. The more water you save, the fewer dams will be built. This means less damage to the environment and to animal habitats.

Cut the plastic rings that package six-packs of drinks. Seabirds and other animals can get their necks caught in the rings and die.

If you only have a short distance to travel, it's fun to walk or ride a bike. That way you notice the things around you and save gasoline and oil at the same time! By saving fuel, you also cut down on pollution.

If everyone in the United States recycled just $^1/_{10}$ of their newspapers, we could save as many as 25 million trees every year. Just think how much animal habitat that would provide!

CANS

BOTTLES

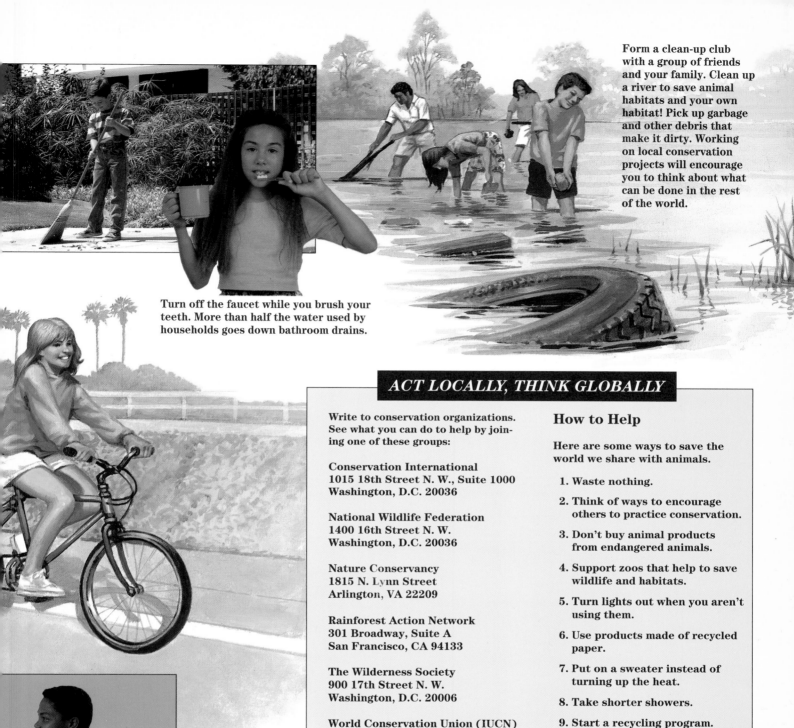

Form a clean-up club with a group of friends and your family. Clean up a river to save animal habitats and your own habitat! Pick up garbage and other debris that make it dirty. Working on local conservation projects will encourage you to think about what can be done in the rest of the world.

Turn off the faucet while you brush your teeth. More than half the water used by households goes down bathroom drains.

ACT LOCALLY, THINK GLOBALLY

Write to conservation organizations. See what you can do to help by joining one of these groups:

Conservation International
1015 18th Street N. W., Suite 1000
Washington, D.C. 20036

National Wildlife Federation
1400 16th Street N. W.
Washington, D.C. 20036

Nature Conservancy
1815 N. Lynn Street
Arlington, VA 22209

Rainforest Action Network
301 Broadway, Suite A
San Francisco, CA 94133

The Wilderness Society
900 17th Street N. W.
Washington, D.C. 20006

World Conservation Union (IUCN)
1110 Morges
SWITZERLAND

Worldwatch Institute
1776 Massachusetts Avenue, N.W.
Washington, D.C. 20036

World Wildlife Fund
1601 Connecticut Avenue, N.W.
Washington, D.C. 20009

World-Wide Fund for Nature
1250 24th Street, N.W.
Washington, D.C. 20037

How to Help

Here are some ways to save the world we share with animals.

1. Waste nothing.

2. Think of ways to encourage others to practice conservation.

3. Don't buy animal products from endangered animals.

4. Support zoos that help to save wildlife and habitats.

5. Turn lights out when you aren't using them.

6. Use products made of recycled paper.

7. Put on a sweater instead of turning up the heat.

8. Take shorter showers.

9. Start a recycling program.

10. Write to presidents, senators, governors, and other world leaders and ask them to continue current laws and pass new laws that will help clean up the environment and save endangered species.

Index